Contents

What is a dinosaur?

Dinosaurs were reptiles which lived long ago. For many millions of years they lived almost everywhere around the world, but they disappeared 65 million years ago. Dinosaurs lived on the land. They had strong legs and were good walkers or runners. Many were huge, some were small.

Lizards are not dinosaurs, though they are reptiles and are just as old. Lizards are small but very fast and can be fierce. Unlike dinosaurs, the legs of lizards stick out sideways from their body and could never carry the weight of a larger creature. Dinosaurs' legs were positioned directly beneath the body.

Is a lizard a dinosaur?

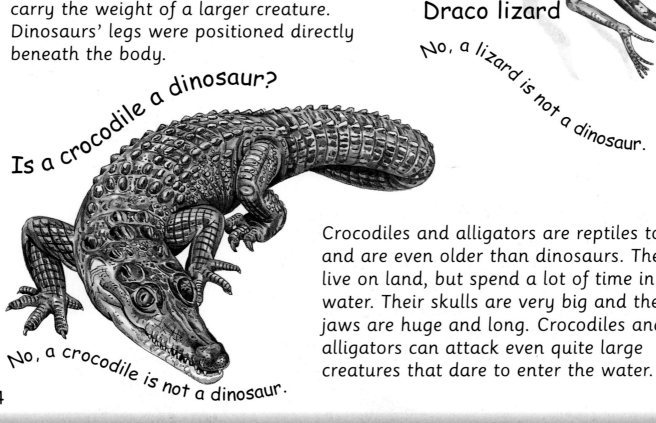

Draco lizard

No, a lizard is not a dinosaur.

Is a crocodile a dinosaur?

No, a crocodile is not a dinosaur.

Crocodiles and alligators are reptiles too and are even older than dinosaurs. They live on land, but spend a lot of time in water. Their skulls are very big and their jaws are huge and long. Crocodiles and alligators can attack even quite large creatures that dare to enter the water.

Scary Creatures
DINOSAURS

Illustrated by
Mark Bergin and
Carolyn Scrace

Created and designed by
David Salariya

Author:

John Cooper is a geologist and Keeper of
the Booth Museum of Natural History in Brighton.
He has studied dinosaurs in Leicestershire and
Sussex in England and at the Carnegie Museum of
Natural History in Pittsburgh, USA. He is the author
of several books on dinosaurs and related subjects.

Artists:

Mark Bergin was born in Hastings in 1961.
He studied at Eastbourne College of Art and has
illustrated many children's non-fiction books. He lives
in Bexhill-on-Sea with his wife and three children.

Carolyn Scrace is a graduate of Brighton
College of Art, England, specialising in design and
illustration. She has worked in animation, advertising
and children's fiction and non-fiction, particularly
natural history.

Additional artist:
Nick Hewetson

Series creator:

David Salariya was born in Dundee,
Scotland. In 1989 he established The Salariya Book
Company. He has illustrated a wide range of books
and has created many new series for publishers in the
UK and overseas. He lives in Brighton with his wife,
illustrator Shirley Willis, and their son.

Editors:

Stephanie Cole
Karen Barker Smith

Photographic credits:

Daniel Heuclin, NHPA: 12
The Natural History Museum, London: 8, 11, 16/17, 26, 27
Kevin Schafer, NHPA: 25
Tom & Therisa Stack, NHPA: 20

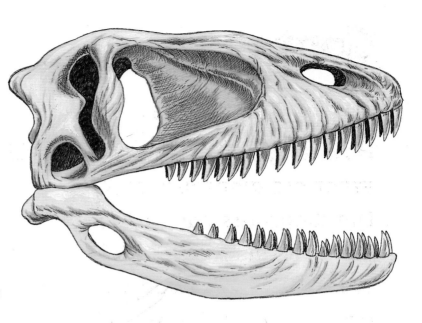

Published in Great Britain in 2002 by
Book House, an imprint of
The Salariya Book Company Ltd
25 Marlborough Place, Brighton BN1 1UB

Visit the Salariya Book Company at
www.salariya.com
www.book-house.co.uk

A catalogue record for this book is available
from the British Library.

ISBN 1 904194 31 1

Printed in Italy.

Printed on paper from sustainable forests.

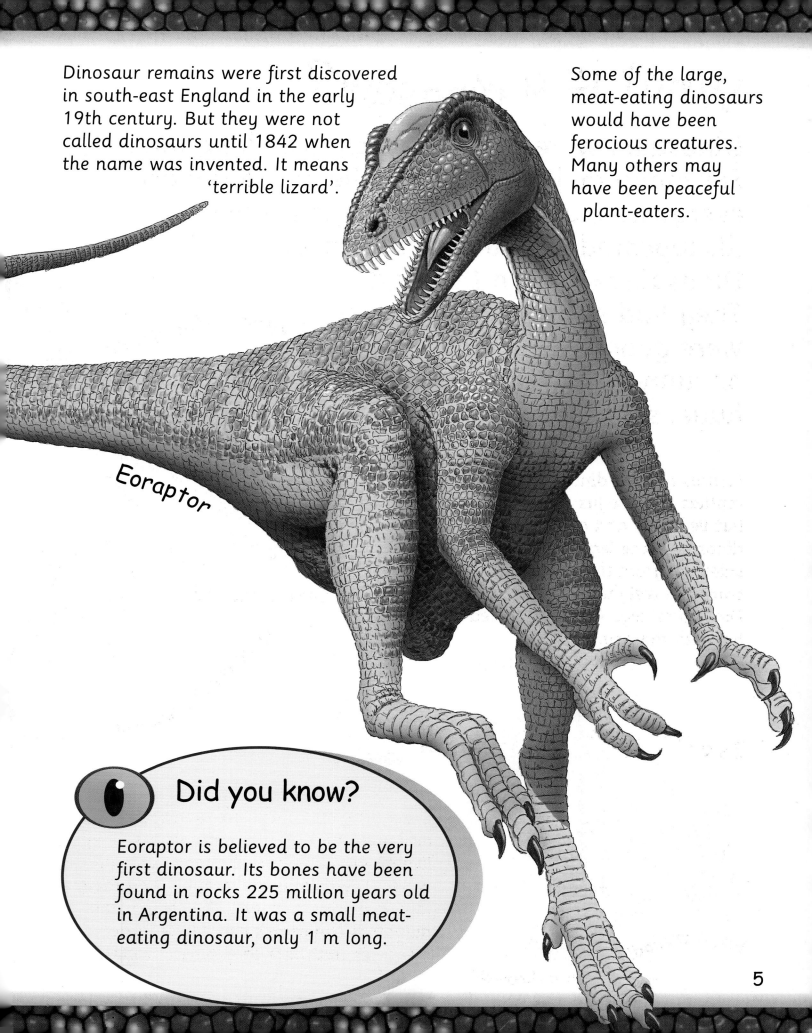

Dinosaur remains were first discovered in south-east England in the early 19th century. But they were not called dinosaurs until 1842 when the name was invented. It means 'terrible lizard'.

Some of the large, meat-eating dinosaurs would have been ferocious creatures. Many others may have been peaceful plant-eaters.

Eoraptor

Did you know?

Eoraptor is believed to be the very first dinosaur. Its bones have been found in rocks 225 million years old in Argentina. It was a small meat-eating dinosaur, only 1 m long.

How long ago did dinosaurs live?

Dinosaurs lived between 225 and 65 million years ago. They lived on Earth for 160 million years! They were not the first reptiles. Before them lived many different types of small lizards. Many of these first reptiles survived to live side-by-side with the dinosaurs. Some, like lizards and crocodiles, still live today.

What did the Earth look like millions of years ago?

Dinosaurs lived so long ago, it is impossible to imagine the passing of so much time. But in all those millions of years the continents, seas, oceans and weather have all changed hugely.

It would be difficult for us to recognise the Earth 200 million years ago. The plants and animals were very different too. We might be able to recognise some of them, but many others are now extinct and are unknown today.

245-208 million years ago

208-135 million years ago

135-65 million years ago

Did you know?

Remains of the earliest known reptile were found in Scotland. It lived 335 million years ago.

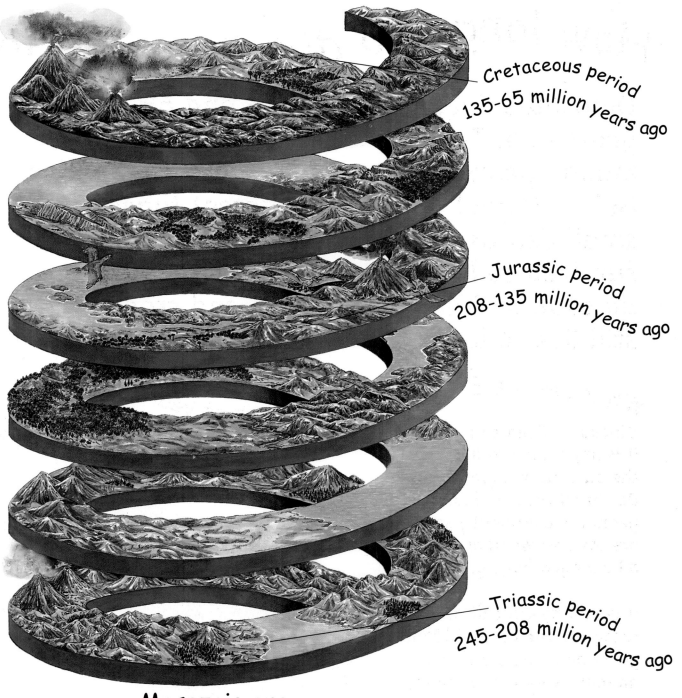

Cretaceous period
135-65 million years ago

Jurassic period
208-135 million years ago

Triassic period
245-208 million years ago

Mesozoic era

The dinosaurs lived in a time known as the Mesozoic era, meaning 'middle life'. This spiral represents the Mesozoic era. The first dinosaurs that we know about were found in rocks about 225 million years old from a period of time called the Triassic.

Scientists believe that most dinosaurs lived in the Jurassic period. There were fewer dinosaurs alive in the Cretaceous period and they became extinct at the end of that period.

What did dinosaurs eat?

Like most creatures alive today, dinosaurs ate either meat or plants. Meat-eating animals are called carnivores. Plant-eating animals are herbivores. Some animals eat both and are called omnivores. There were far more herbivorous dinosaurs than carnivores.

Herbivores have rows of teeth which help grind plant leaves and stems before swallowing. Herbivores are attacked by meat-eaters, so they often have horns for protection, like this Triceratops (below).

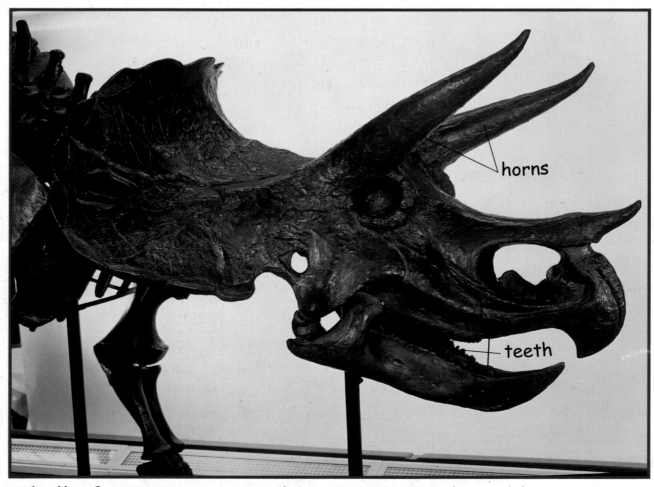

horns

teeth

Skull of a Triceratops showing its teeth and horns

Stegosaurus was a herbivore that lived in the Jurassic period in North America. It had bony plates on its back and spines on its tail for protection. Stegosaurus was probably a very gentle creature. It depended on its armour plating, rather than speed, to escape attacks.

Stegosaurus

gastroliths

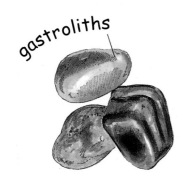

Stegosauruses, like many dinosaurs, swallowed stones to help their stomachs grind plant food to paste. These stones are called gastroliths.

Plateosaurus lived at the end of the Triassic period. It was one of the first large dinosaurs, about 7 m long and weighing 2 tonnes. The shape of its jaw and its rows of ridged teeth show that it was a herbivore. It might have been able to stand on its back legs and eat leaves that were out of the reach of other dinosaurs.

Plateosaurus

Did dinosaurs eat each other?

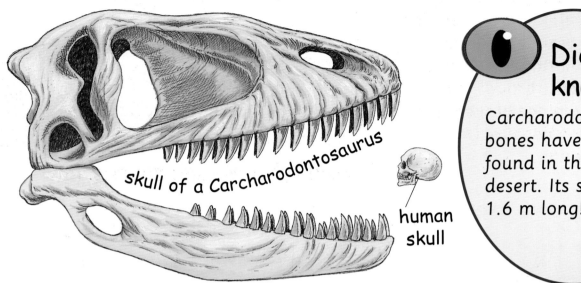

skull of a Carcharodontosaurus

human skull

Carnivorous dinosaurs needed to eat meat to live. The best source of meat was other dinosaurs! Smaller dinosaurs may have caught lizards and insects. Others may have eaten fish.

All the meat-eaters had large, sharp, pointed teeth. They usually had far fewer teeth than the herbivores.

The teeth of Tyrannosaurus were up to 20 cm long. Only a small part of the tooth would have been seen above the gum. Each tooth had an edge like a saw, which made it perfect for slicing through meat.

Tyrannosaurus

Megalosaurus was the first dinosaur to be named and was found in England in the early 1800s. Its teeth were perfect for a carnivore: long, sharp and backward-pointing. Dinosaurs grew new teeth throughout their life to replace broken and lost ones. Megalosaurus was about 9 m long.

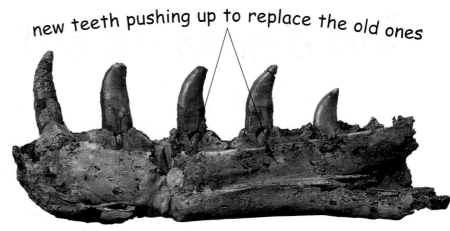

new teeth pushing up to replace the old ones

Part of a Megalosaurus jaw

Tyrannosaurus was 12 m long

Albertosaurus was 9 m long

Daspletosaurus was 9 m long

Did dinosaurs lay eggs?

The first dinosaur eggs ever found were discovered in Mongolia in 1923. They are about the size of a large potato and are believed to be from the small dinosaur Protoceratops. Since then many more dinosaur eggs have been found. Because most reptiles lay eggs, scientists think that most dinosaurs laid eggs too.

Dinosaur nesting colony

Fossilised dinosaur nests full of eggs have been found in Mongolia and Canada. Most seem to have been simply scooped out of the ground. Perhaps soft vegetation lined these nests. Many have been found together in nesting colonies.

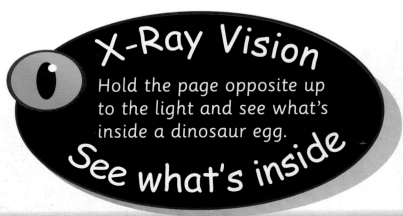

Fossilised dinosaur eggs

Dinosaur eggs can be different shapes. Some are long and oval, others are almost perfectly round. It is often not known what type of dinosaur laid the eggs. In some eggs, the fossils of the tiny young dinosaurs have also been found.

X-Ray Vision

Hold the page opposite up to the light and see what's inside a dinosaur egg.

See what's inside

Were dinosaurs good parents?

Newly hatched dinosaurs were tiny compared to their parents. The bones of some baby dinosaurs were too weak to support them at first. The parents must have protected them until they were strong enough to leave the nest. Other types of baby dinosaurs probably hatched ready to leave the nest straightaway.

Maiasaura parent feeding its young

Skeletons of baby Maiasaura dinosaurs have been found in nests in Montana, USA. Their teeth were worn down. This must mean that their parents fed them while still in the nest.

The Maiasaura nests found in Montana were about 7 m apart from each other. This was about the same length as an adult, so each parent sitting on a nest was just far enough away from its neighbours. This also means that egg-stealing animals could not easily attack the nests.

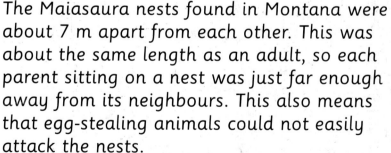

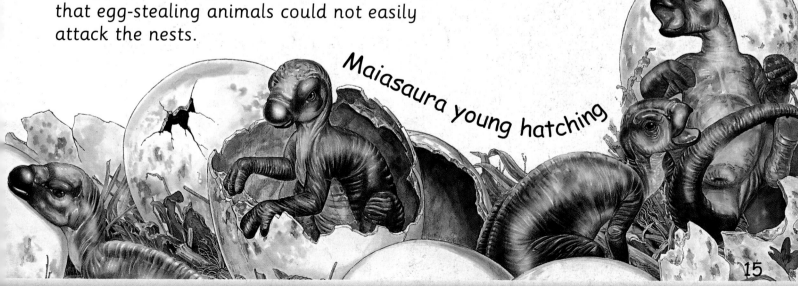

Maiasaura young hatching

How big were dinosaurs?

Dinosaurs were the biggest land-living animals on Earth. The biggest of all were a group of dinosaurs called the sauropods. Sauropod skeletons have been found all over the world. They were huge four-legged plant-eaters with small heads, massive bodies and long necks and tails. The best known are Brachiosaurus, Apatosaurus and Diplodocus.

This skeleton of a Shunosaurus was found in China where it lived about 160 million years ago. It was almost 10 m long and 3 m tall. Later sauropods had longer necks and longer tails. Shunosaurus had only 12 vertebrae in its neck.

Shunosaurus

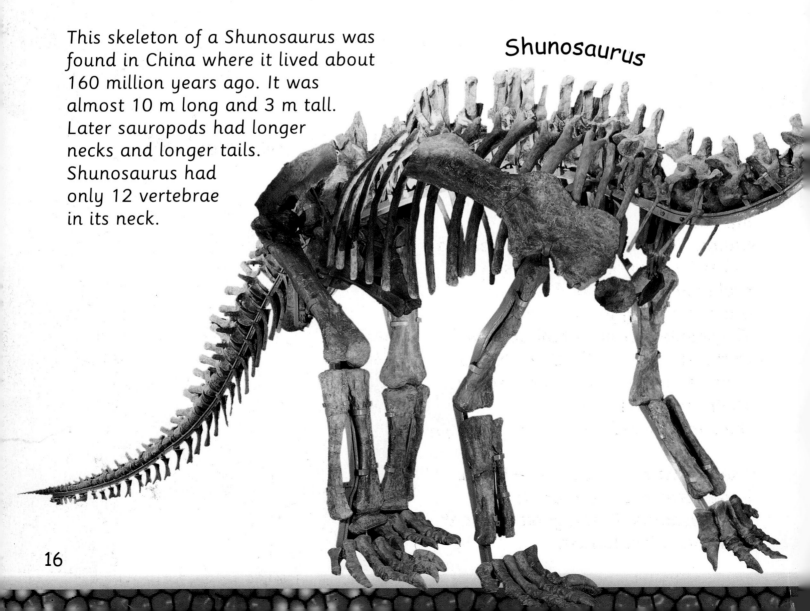

Mamenchisaurus had the longest neck of all the dinosaurs. It had 19 vertebrae. Mamenchisaurus might have used its neck to feed on the ground in wide arcs, without having to move its body.

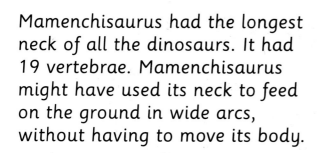

vertebrae

Mamenchisaurus

Modern-day elephant

Although dinosaurs were very large animals, they had very small brains. The smallest brains belonged to the herbivorous dinosaurs, who probably relied on their size or armour plating for protection. The smallest brains of all belonged to the stegosaurs like Stegosaurus, Kentrosaurus and Huayangosaurus. Their brains were about the size of a walnut!

The largest brains belonged to the huge carnivorous dinosaurs like Albertosaurus. It had good eyesight and was a fast hunter.

Stegosaurus

Did dinosaurs live in water?

Dinosaurs evolved to live on land. They did not live in the water, though they probably enjoyed cooling off in a river or lake. But living at the same time as the dinosaurs were other reptiles that could only live in the water. These included the plesiosaurs and ichthyosaurs.

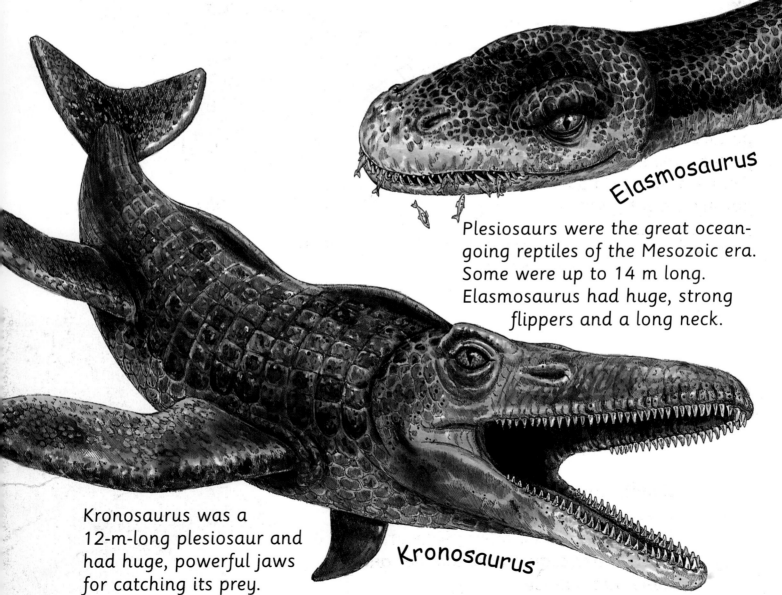

Elasmosaurus

Plesiosaurs were the great ocean-going reptiles of the Mesozoic era. Some were up to 14 m long. Elasmosaurus had huge, strong flippers and a long neck.

Kronosaurus was a 12-m-long plesiosaur and had huge, powerful jaws for catching its prey.

Kronosaurus

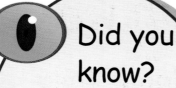
A fossilised ichthyosaur was found with the skeleton of its baby half in and half out of its body. This shows that they gave birth to live young, just like whales do today.

The ichthyosaurs were the dolphins and porpoises of the Mesozoic era. They were well adapted for swimming fast and hunting fish. They had powerful tails, streamlined bodies and huge eyes. The earliest ichthyosaurs lived around 200 million years ago and survived right to the end of the Cretaceous period, when the dinosaurs also died out.

Ichthyosaurus lived in waters near Europe and North America in the Jurassic and Cretaceous periods. Hundreds of complete fossils have been found. Only 2 m long, it had powerful front paddles for steering and a large tail.

Ichthyosaurus

ribs

spine

Shonisaurus

Shonisaurus was the largest of the ichthyosaurs at 15 m long. It lived in the Triassic period in North America. Later ichthyosaurs were smaller and more streamlined.

Did dinosaurs fly?

None of the dinosaurs could fly. The first group of backboned animals that learned to fly was the pterosaurs. These reptiles flew with wings made of skin. They first appear as fossils from late in the Triassic period, about 230 million years ago. The first birds appeared in the Jurassic period. Scientists believe that birds evolved from early forms of feathered dinosaurs.

bony crest

Pteranodon was one of the larger pterosaurs. Its fossils have been found in Europe and North America. It had a short body, no tail and a curious bony crest on its head. No one knows what the crest was for. Pteranodon probably glided over the oceans.

Pteranodon

wings of skin

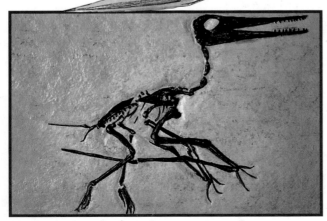

Pterodactylus was a small pterosaur common in Europe and Africa. There were many different types, but none of them had a wingspan of more than 75 cm. Pterodactylus kochi had long narrow jaws with many sharp teeth. It probably skimmed over the sea and grabbed small fish with its open jaws.

Fossilised Pterodactylus kochi

Did dinosaurs have feathers?

Newly discovered fossils from China show that some small, early dinosaurs were covered in feathers. These creatures did not have wings and were not birds. The feathers possibly evolved to keep the animals warm. These small meat-eating dinosaurs had hollow bones so that they weighed less. This was perfect for running fast and for early attempts at flying! Many scientists now think of birds as modern dinosaurs.

Yes, some dinosaurs had feathers.

Quetzalcoatlus

Archaeopteryx

The earliest known bird is called Archaeopteryx. It was discovered in Germany in 1860. It lived in the Jurassic period, about 160 million years ago.

Several Archaeopteryx remains have been found, including some single feathers. Its skeleton is almost identical to a small carnivorous dinosaur called Compsognathus. Only the feathers show it was a bird.

Albertosaurus

Large carnivores like Albertosaurus could probably run quickly for short distances. They could have reached 40 kilometres per hour.

How fast were dinosaurs?

Corythosaurus

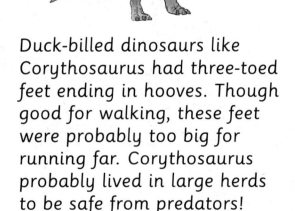

Duck-billed dinosaurs like Corythosaurus had three-toed feet ending in hooves. Though good for walking, these feet were probably too big for running far. Corythosaurus probably lived in large herds to be safe from predators!

The feet of large sauropods (below) were made for supporting their huge weight not for running. These dinosaurs' size and powerful tail was enough to put off most attackers.

Scientists study dinosaur skeletons to try and work out their walking and running speeds. Also, the distance between footprints left by a running dinosaur can be measured to show its speed. Carnivores could catch prey by running fast. Herbivores could escape them by trying to run even faster!

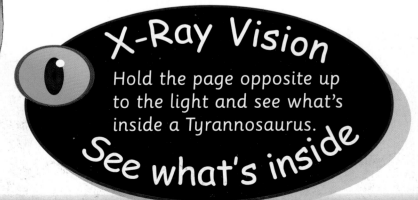

X-Ray Vision

Hold the page opposite up to the light and see what's inside a Tyrannosaurus.

See what's inside

Tyrannosaurus

skull

sharp teeth

ribs

vertebrae

thigh bone

claws

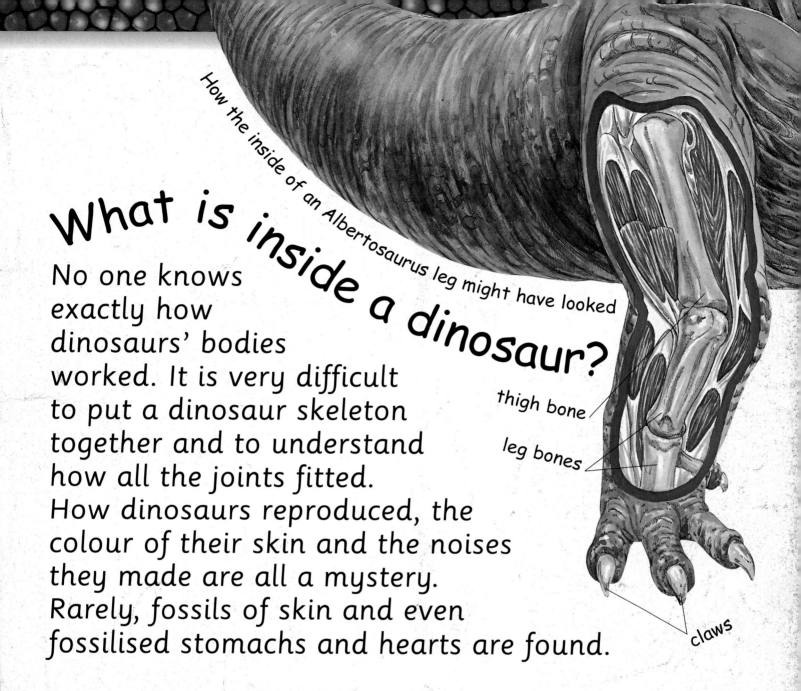

How the inside of an Albertosaurus leg might have looked

thigh bone

leg bones

claws

What is inside a dinosaur?

No one knows exactly how dinosaurs' bodies worked. It is very difficult to put a dinosaur skeleton together and to understand how all the joints fitted. How dinosaurs reproduced, the colour of their skin and the noises they made are all a mystery. Rarely, fossils of skin and even fossilised stomachs and hearts are found.

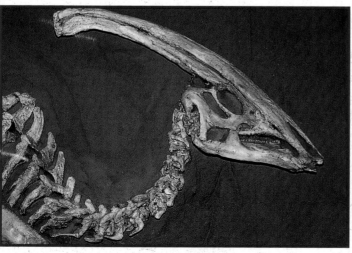

Fossilised Parasauralophus skeleton

Dinosaur fossils are almost always the remains of hard body parts – bones (left), teeth, eggshells and gastroliths. It is very rare to find fossils of soft body parts because they rot away. Scientists use their knowledge of modern reptiles to work out what the muscles and internal organs of dinosaurs were like.

How do we know about dinosaurs?

Everything we know about dinosaurs comes from fossils found in the last 200 years. When bones are discovered they have to be carefully dug up. They are then taken to museums where scientists slowly remove the rock from around them using hammers and chisels or pneumatic and electric instruments.

Did you know?

A complete Tyrannosaurus skeleton, dug up in South Dakota, USA, was sold in 1997 for over five million pounds! It was thought that the dinosaur was female – it was named Sue after the person who discovered it.

Dinosaur fossils are found in rocks all over the world. These two scientists (left) are working on the bones of a sauropod dinosaur being excavated in the Sahara desert, Niger. They are strengthening weak areas of the bone with plaster.

Scientists excavating a dinosaur fossil

Fossils: from earth to museum

A fossilised bone is found and exposed by scraping away the rock around it.

As the bone dries in the air it may need to be painted with resin to protect the surface.

The exposed bone is covered in plaster. This hardens and protects the bone.

The bone is removed from the ground and the plaster is completed.

When bones have been identified, artists illustrate how they might join together.

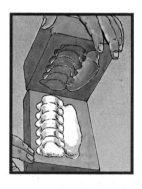

Rubber moulds are made of the bones. The moulds are then used to make copies of them.

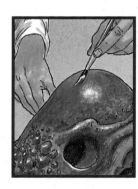

The copies are painted to exactly match the original bones and the originals are safely stored.

The final stages might involve mounting the bones on a steel frame. Most modern dinosaur skeletons on display are made from lightweight copies of real bones. These are much easier to handle and not as fragile or valuable. This scientist (right) is applying the finishing touches to a Massospondylus skeleton found in southern Africa.

Mounting a skeleton in a laboratory 27

What happened to dinosaurs?

Sixty-five million years ago, something extraordinary happened to the Earth. Scientists believe a huge asteroid hit the planet, plunging into the sea near the coast of Mexico. Scientists have found a crater beneath the seabed, 180 km across. The asteroid was perhaps 10 km wide and hit the Earth at a speed of 100,000 kph.

The effects of this impact would have included dust in the atmosphere, volcanoes and earthquakes, enormous tidal waves, high winds and storms.

As the skies became full of dust, amazing sunsets would appear. Soon, the sun would disappear from view, perhaps for many months. It would become very cold. Most plants, which normally need sunshine to live, would die.

The plant-eating dinosaurs would soon begin to suffer from the lack of food. In a few weeks they would begin to starve and die. Smaller reptiles, small mammals and insects might survive because they needed less food.

The carnivorous dinosaurs might feast on dead and dying herbivores. But once they were all gone, the carnivores too would die. Soon many types of animals, including all the dinosaurs, would be dead.

When the dust cleared, sunlight would reappear. Tiny animals such as earthworms, shrews and insects would have survived by scavenging. Bigger animals, including crocodiles, snakes and frogs, would come out of hibernation. Seeds buried in the ground would be warmed and grow. Slowly the world would return to normal, but without the dinosaurs.

Dinosaur facts

Scientists have studied fossilised dinosaur droppings from Montana, USA. The droppings contain a lot of wood fibres from trees. It seems that at least some herbivorous dinosaurs could eat very tough wood.

In one dinosaur nesting colony that has been found, 19 eggs were carefully arranged in a spiral inside the nests. Each nest had been simply scooped out of the ground.

Argentinosaurus is only known from the few leg bones and vertebrae that have been found. It was much bigger than any other dinosaur, perhaps up to 40 m long!

The largest known carnivorous dinosaur is Giganotosaurus from Argentina. It was 16 m long and weighed more than 8 tonnes.

Skeletons of the small carnivorous dinosaur Coelophysis found in New Mexico were discovered to have the skeletons of young Coelophysis inside their bodies. They were cannibals!

A nest of eggs in Mongolia was found together with a skeleton of a dinosaur called Oviraptor. It was once thought that Oviraptor was stealing and eating the eggs. Now scientists think that the Oviraptor died in a sandstorm while sitting on the nest trying to protect its own eggs.

Baryonyx was the first fish-eating dinosaur discovered. Its remains were found in Surrey, England, in 1983 with the fossils of fish left in its stomach. Baryonyx had long jaws like a crocodile and huge claws to help it catch its prey.

When scientists carefully studied a number of different carnivorous dinosaurs, they discovered that about a quarter of the animals had fractures to their hands and feet. These may have happened when attacking other dinosaurs for food. Though probably painful for a while, such fractures would usually have healed themselves eventually.

Glossary

aggressive Something which shows fierceness.

carnivore Any animal that eats the flesh of other animals as its main food.

cold-blooded An animal whose body temperature changes according to the temperature of its surroundings.

Cretaceous The period of time that began about 135 million years ago and ended about 65 million years ago.

evolve To change in some way over a very long period of time.

excavate To find buried objects by digging them up.

extinct Species of animals that are no longer alive anywhere in the world.

fossil The very old remains of a plant or animal.

gastrolith A stone or pebble swallowed by an animal and kept in its gut. Gastroliths help to grind up tough food.

herbivore Any animal that eats plant material as its main food.

Jurassic The period of time that began about 208 million years ago and ended about 135 million years ago.

nesting colony An area where lots of the same type of animal make nests and have young.

pneumatic A machine that works by using compressed air.

predator An animal that hunts other living creatures for food.

prey Animals that are hunted by other animals for food.

reptile A cold-blooded animal that breathes with lungs.

Triassic The period of time that began about 245 million years ago and ended about 208 million years ago.

vertebrae The bones that fit together to form an animal's spine.

wingspan The distance measured between the wing tips of a bird.

Index